AF533449

Érika Freire
Aguinaldo C. Surdi

# Body, Playfulness and Education

Érika Freire
Aguinaldo C. Surdi

# Body, Playfulness and Education

## Thinking about Early Childhood Physical Education

ScienciaScripts

**Imprint**
Any brand names and product names mentioned in this book are subject to trademark, brand or patent protection and are trademarks or registered trademarks of their respective holders. The use of brand names, product names, common names, trade names, product descriptions etc. even without a particular marking in this work is in no way to be construed to mean that such names may be regarded as unrestricted in respect of trademark and brand protection legislation and could thus be used by anyone.

Cover image: www.ingimage.com

This book is a translation from the original published under ISBN 978-3-330-19632-2.

Publisher:
Sciencia Scripts
is a trademark of
Dodo Books Indian Ocean Ltd. and OmniScriptum S.R.L publishing group

120 High Road, East Finchley, London, N2 9ED, United Kingdom
Str. Armeneasca 28/1, office 1, Chisinau MD-2012, Republic of Moldova, Europe
Printed at: see last page
**ISBN: 978-620-8-21534-7**

Copyright © Érika Freire, Aguinaldo C. Surdi
Copyright © 2024 Dodo Books Indian Ocean Ltd. and OmniScriptum S.R.L publishing group

## SUMMARY

# PRESENTATION

The book "Body, Playfulness and Education: Thinking about Children's Physical Education" is a collection of texts that aims to discuss children's physical education, focusing on the body that plays as a key component of children's sensitive education.

In the first text, "Body and sensitive knowledge: some approximations with education", a theoretical reflection on the body and sensitive knowledge was developed. It emphasizes the importance of sensitive education as a new way of thinking about learning and education. The aim is for each subject to be able to perceive difference, the other and with the other. Learning in diversity is rooted in corporeality.

The second text, "Playing and children's physical education: a report of a pedagogical experience at the UFRN's children's education center (NEI)", presents important considerations about the meaning of playing at school, as well as its pedagogical conception, highlighting this experience as a process in human formation.

The third text, "Physical education in early childhood education: capoeira - an intertwining of knowledge", seeks to reflect on the pedagogical practice of the body in movement in the school space, as well as the role of Physical Education as a culture of movement.

The text on "Le parkour and physical education: a bodily practice of movement culture for children" presented and contextualized the history of the sport of Le Parkour - a bodily practice of adventure - as the content of the movement workshop, and the relationship with a conception of the body, culture and nature.

The organizers

# 1 THE BODY AND SENSITIVE KNOWLEDGE: SOME APPROACHES TO EDUCATION

Aguinaldo Cesar Surdi Professor at DEF/UFRN.aguinaldosurdi@yahoo.com.br

Erika Janaina Santiago Moreira Freire Master's student PPGEF-UFRN/NEI.erikafreire@outlook.com.br

Josd Pereira de Mello Professor at DEF/UFRN.jose.pereira.melo@uol.com.br

## INTRODUCTION

The loss of sensitivity in the human race probably began at the dawn of Western civilization, with the advent of the discovery of reason, which was initiated by the Greeks. The overcoming of myths by the new "rational thinking" provided an early "way" of understanding our reality. This new possibility gradually asserted itself and became the only reliable and accepted way to arrive at a truth about the things of the world. Thus, within this same context, the disenchantment of the world began. The rational and measurable world must find a way to achieve this goal and, on the way, it has to get rid of many things that "get in the way" of the search for truth. Among the readings and the relapse of the world that have gradually been eliminated, one of them is that which makes use of sensibility.

As rational beings, we have to deprive ourselves of our privileged possibility of feeling because it can lead us down a dark path in the face of the clarity of the so-called absolute truths proposed by rational thought. These truths have turned the world into a machine, in which people are just tiny cogs that differ from each other only by means of a number. Here we have clear rules to follow in order to achieve results that meet measurable objectives. We have become automatons, lifeless beings, without humility, compassion, joy or happiness. We are ashamed to cry, to say that we love, to really be what we were born to be, because, after all, we are human and sensitive beings.

Western thought denies the senses as a source of apprehension of the world. It then created the concept of truth, based on reason as the paradigm of knowledge. Knowing has thus become the direction towards what is true, which seeks to judge life and not interpret it. Judging life requires artifices and cause and effect procedures, which should lead to predictable results and determinants. Interpreting life takes into account human beings and their differences: beings who have a history and who are unpredictable. As such, they are capable of producing new interpretations and adjusting in different ways to countless situations. Santin (1992) challenges this modern view, asking how can we research life or the phenomenology of the living? How can its message be deciphered? He points out that the modern model of knowledge production practiced by scientific methods of confrontation between subject and object and mathematical reading can in no way decipher the totality of the language of corporeality. For the author, this knowledge must be made directly, without the mediation of the laws and rules of scientific rationality, but based on the lived world of each person. The aim of this text is to reflect on the relationship between the body, education and sensitive knowledge, emphasizing the importance of this relationship in contributing to a more global and meaningful education that takes human sensitivity into account.

## BODY, EDUCATION AND SENSITIVE KNOWLEDGE

At this point, we want to argue in favor of the body as an experiential and perceptive possibility, essential for education and sensitive knowledge. The body is the essential condition for the sensible language of the world. It is through the body that our presence is made in the world and thus we can understand it and give it meaning. Our existence is realized in the body (MERLEAU-PONTY, 1999). Modern life tries to silence body language. However close modernity comes to achieving this goal, there is always hope. This hope lies in investing in an education in sensitivity. For this to happen, the body has to come into play, because, according to Santin (1994, p.91), "corporeality is man's way of being" as a total and unique being, characterized by playfulness. But... Where do we find the playful body? According to the author, in children, who do non-productive things. They don't think about the result, they simply do, feeling pleasure and joy, as long as they have access to the freedom that allows them to dream, invent, imagine and create new worlds.

The body is able to perceive and thus feel the world in a broader way and before our traditional mental processes which tend to reduce it to concepts and schemes, simplifying what will always be unlimited for our corporeality. We can make a distinction between the intelligible and the sensible or, according to Duarte Junior (2001), knowing and feeling. Knowing translates into that knowledge which is treated abstractly by our brain. In this exercise, logical signs are produced, such as words and numbers. Sensing, on the other hand, corresponds to the knowledge present in the human body and manifests itself in a variety of situations which, as the author exemplifies, in activities such as:

> [...] balance as a form that allows us to ride a bicycle, the harmonious movement of the hands as they make different rhythms sound on a percussion instrument, the precise pass of a soccer player who places the ball on the chest of a teammate thirty meters away with his feet, or even the stomach's refusal to accept spoiled food based on our sense of smell. Knowing, then, is only mental, intellectual, whereas knowing also resides in the flesh, in the organism as a whole, in a union of body and mind (p. 125).

The body always knows what to do, all that is needed, according to Santin (1987), is to decipher body language. The body as a communicative medium goes through countless interpretative possibilities that enable the constitution of new intersubjectivities and experiences in the lived space. The body thus goes beyond its physiology and its own self. For this to happen, our sensitivity must be accurate. Our bodily intuition projects us to solve problems or issues before we think about them. However, because we are too rational, intelligible - scientifically proven - solutions have more meaning. We look for rational concepts and definitions, which often don't offer the best solutions. As a result, our sensitivity to feeling body language deteriorates until it disappears altogether. This body knowledge brings us face to face with reality, providing us with a path of broad wisdom that doesn't require mental development, a calculated and designed strategy to solve or do something. Our daily actions are basically based on our bodily knowledge and not on elaborate, intellectualized knowledge, such as how to distinguish smells, tastes, sounds and textures (DUARTE JUNIOR, 2001). To illustrate this, we cite the fable of the centipede, which was asked how it managed to organize itself and not confuse the movement of all those legs. Since it had never thought about it, from then on it began to fall over in an attempt to mentally organize its bodily knowledge, the knowledge that makes its legs always move harmoniously. This bodily knowledge differs from mental schematizations in that it aims for completeness, and for this it has no specific method. It takes into account all the factors that are present in that experience and defines a harmony that can only be expressed and manifested bodily. However, I believe that both knowing/intelligible and knowing/sensible are different forms, but important for the life of the human being. The problem lies in the overly accentuated way in which these possibilities of knowing and feeling the world have been separated and the value given to rational and abstract knowledge. Both have their meaning of being, but the issue is that one disputes the dominance of the world through the construction of criteria and methods to arrive at absolute truth, excluding other ways of knowing and knowing, while the other just wants its space to maintain the human side of man with pleasure and joy. These different and important possibilities that we are currently witnessing are very clear in a passage by Alves (1998), when he comments that:

> What separates us from the animals is that the thoughts that live in our heads have started to proliferate, multiply and grow. This has had undeniable advantages because it was thanks to the thoughts that live in our heads that the human world was built. Philosophy, science, technology... They've grown so much that they've clogged up the body's wisdom. Knowledge grows, sedimenting, layer upon layer, and there comes a time when we forget the wordless wisdom that lives in the body.

Therefore, this forgotten wisdom, endowed with sensitivity and expressed bodily, needs a more important place in our lives. This knowledge enables us to deal with a world that is always in the making, where we can leave our mark. Our bodily action provides the meaning and sense of the world, because only it is capable of feeling and perceiving all the vibrations, relationships and feelings that take place between us and the world. This first contact is sensitive and fundamental for the world to have more meaning for us, according to our convictions. Thus, everyday knowledge, or even common sense, is fundamental as a primary source of any knowledge and should be valued. Damasio (1996), through his research, discovered that the separation between body and mind makes no sense. All knowledge, even the most abstract, has its origin in the sensory processes of the body. Merleau-Ponty (1999) also defends the idea that all scientific knowledge is based on sensible knowledge, because our body and the world are linked as an indivisible substance.

The sensitivity that is present in our body allows it to be the primary source of meaning, in other words, we construct a world by making sense of it. Thus, "producing meaning, interpreting significance, is not a purely cognitive activity, or even an intellectual or cerebral one, it is the body, this lake of our sensibilities, which signifies, which interprets." (PARRET *apud* DUARTE JUNIOR 2001, p.128). Sensitive knowledge places us before the world as a bodily being who interprets and signifies the world in order to make sense of our experiences and, consequently, our existence. In this sense, Santin (1994) emphasizes that it is in corporeality that man's humanness is characterized, in his relationship with others and with the world. "The assertion that corporeality characterizes the specifically human aspect of man's existence does not mean that it is reduced to the individual body. On the contrary, the idea of corporeality implies a link not only with other bodies, but also with the world." (p. 97).

Sensitive knowledge consists of feeling life fully and then thinking about it. This path could be included in an education for sensitivity, encouraging the education of looking, listening, tasting, smelling and touching. Through direct contact with the wonders that make up the world, the possibility is created for everyone to produce their own "truths", which are different from scientific truths, based on statistical evidence and generalizations. Truths that have "an individual and proper character, particular and inherent to the existence of a human subject, small, flawed and limited, but great in its awareness of the cosmos. A subject without whom no scientific truth would exist" (DUARTE JUNIOR, 2001 p.132). Therefore, this knowledge is in our daily lives and manifests itself bodily. Our body is able to capture the complexity of the world with the right quality of detail, such as sounds, smells, images, buildings, other people and everything else that makes up the world and gives us the pleasure of living.

The education of sensitive knowledge has become essential nowadays and must try to prevent the increase in the unilateral and uniform view of the world that contemporary man has due to the scientific-technological impact. A globalized and humane view of the world must be restored and sensitive knowledge becomes fundamental to this process. An education based on sensitive knowledge offers man a power that is gradually constituted and allows him to give too much importance to some more restricted fields of knowledge and, consequently, to forget about them, thus integrating man with himself, with others and with society. Among the possibilities for educating the sensitive, art can make a special contribution, developing and promoting perceptions and feelings of the reality experienced. Relating this to the school environment, Duarte Junior comments that these perceptions and feelings should be based on the students' personal experiences and reflections. Another fundamental issue in this educational process is teacher training. We don't want to go into detail about this here, but we do want to emphasize that teachers must also have and know how to deal with this sensitive knowledge. They must give importance to the particularities and details of the world around them, broadening their scope of action to include the sensory and bodily domains that make up their existence. They must build knowledge and practices that are linked to real everyday situations, teaching and learning from the diverse cultures and knowledge that each student brings with them to the classroom. In this sense, teachers' relationships with their knowledge will be in constant transformation. We know, therefore, that our industrial society defines the type of education we should have. Thus, the economic market demands that people be trained to work. This market-based education, marked by technical, instrumental and useful knowledge, stifles the initiatives of schools and teachers who want to enable an education of the sensible. Some of the characteristics that make an education for sensitivity possible are already present in the Curriculum Guidelines for Primary and Secondary Education (1999). In the guidelines, we see the following paragraphs that strengthen sensitive knowledge, such as: "The exercise of creativity and respect for the democratic order; the ethical principles of sensitivity, creativity and the diversity of artistic and cultural manifestations"; "[....] introduce projects and activities of interest to their communities [...]"; "[...] the aesthetics of sensitivity should replace repetition and standardization, stimulating creativity, inventiveness, curiosity about the unusual, affectivity [...]". Even so, this is not enough to reach the hearts of teachers and principals who, perhaps because they don't have a more sensitive upbringing, have let their hearts harden and can only perceive knowledge as something methodical and regulated, with an industrial utility.

As we've already mentioned, the crisis is intensified by the growing distance between sensible and intelligible knowledge. In the educational system, this separation is very evident in the proliferation of technical courses and basic courses to prepare for the job market. They are basically instrumental and aim to provide simplified knowledge that can be used quickly in companies, such as providing services, helping in the automation and mechanics sectors and other jobs that fit perfectly into the modern industrialization process. Therefore, education must be instrumental, providing the intellectual tools for people to work and, consequently, produce. They must be able to read, write and, above all, be proficient in mathematics. The education practiced in many schools today is conditioned to this. Many of them already start this process in kindergarten. This priority on intelligible and rational knowledge distances people from the breadth, depth and complexity of the world. There is a saying: "What is essential is invisible to the eye". We can say that this essentiality is found neither in the world nor in man, but in their most intimate relationship, which is felt. Human reason must broaden, it must encompass more and better. It must not remain solely instrumental, but open up to other forms of knowledge. This reason that characterizes the human being "needs to mean more, much more; it needs to encompass all the knowledge provided by human aesthesia, by the sensible apprehension of the world, which, recalling Merleau-Ponty, is also revealed as the construction of meaning." (DUARTE JUNIOR, 2001, p.173). The education of the sensible, because it is related to experience and meaning, acts in the aesthetic dimension. According to Nunes & Rego (2011, p.103-104):

The aesthetic dimension establishes a fruitful space for sensitization in the process of re-signification and in the constitution of new subjectivities, an interpretation that establishes new discursive domains and produces meanings according to an aesthetic of existence. Learning, seen from this perspective, enables the generation of environments that lead to the production of knowledge through action and reflection on the processes that make it up, exposes a corporeal knowledge based on the recovery of the human condition and the intersubjective construction of meaning, and dissipates any dichotomy that may exist between reason and emotion. The sharing of meanings and the creation of senses generate intersubjectivities that produce new and important spaces for action.

In the education of the sensible, the body is fundamental as an existential field that can contemplate and absorb the limitless. It encompasses the intelligible and the sensible, and goes beyond. It enables new meanings and re-significances that transcend the relationship of space and time, as it allows for the reinterpretation of issues that have already been analyzed under other approaches. Corporeality thus opens up a space for sensitizing the world, linking individual time-space and collectively instituted time-space in a movement in which the subject interprets himself, the other and the world. Santin (1994) emphasizes pleasure as a dynamic of corporeality. "Pleasure possesses a dynamism that can be identified as the principle of desire." (p.99). Pleasure manifests itself as a consequence for corporeality to happen harmoniously. "Desire activates the search for situations of pleasure and inaugurates the very life of corporeality." (p.99). This process manifests itself as a single, indivisible being. Pleasure, desire and corporeality are part of a whole that the author calls "desiring corporeality." (p. 100). This corporeality becomes fundamental in the process of educating sensitivity, through the power of giving. We give ourselves bodily to the world for the pleasure that this relationship makes possible. We are encouraged all the time to live and thus perceive and feel the old ways of seeing the world in different ways.

In this way, education must prepare for the instability of the world, learning about itself and from itself in order to try to understand the world. "To think through passion, to be seduced by discovery and to rediscover oneself in the face of it. Interrogate, question, doubt and set off, even if you don't know what you're going to find." (NUNES & REGO, 2011, p.98). Interpretations of events must be based on the diversity of experiences that are not acquired, but lived bodily. Meaningful experiences make us lose control and become completely involved with things in the world. This strength is fundamental for a solid and deeper learning of the possibilities that life offers us to live more fully and happily.

These bodily experiences can be exemplified in the following way: when we plan a trip, for example, we gradually start to think about it and, the closer the date gets, the more we think about it and organize ourselves. We plan ahead, we create expectations. When the trip begins, unforeseen circumstances arise and we have to improvise various solutions along the way. Therefore, knowledge requires, as one of the preparations for a trip, the acceptance of the unexpected or, even, of what is to come, of what we haven't thought of and which is beyond our control (NUNES & REGO, 2011). Serres (1993, p.40) comments that "[...] learning opens up in the body a place for mestigagens, to be filled by other people".

## FINAL CONSIDERATIONS

Sensitive education enables a new way of thinking about learning and education. It emphasizes that each subject is able to perceive difference, the other and with the other. Learning in diversity is rooted in corporeality. In this way, it is an embodied knowledge that requires a new ethical paradigm that involves corporeality and subjectivities at the heart of the educational process. A knowledge that creates spaces for sensitization and re-signification of the world, constituting bundles of possibilities, axes of coexistence.

The importance of educating the senses becomes clear when we turn our attention to the possibilities of perceiving reality as a social construction, in which the meaning of the countless forms of manifestation of touching, looking, smelling, tasting, talking and the other, in other words, feeling, intensifies. Being attentive to these signs can bring more meaning to one's existence, open us up to the knowledge of the body and to an expressive and transformative experience, which we believe is fundamental in our current educational process. Therefore, investing in an education of the sensitive, as well as contributing to the development of people who are fuller and more complete in their relationship with the world, also contributes to the creation of human principles on which we can develop new parameters of knowledge, for the most fundamental knowledge, that is, knowing how to live.

## BIBLIOGRAPHICAL REFERENCES

ALVES, R. **Concerto for body and soul**. Sao Paulo, Papirus, 1998.

DUARTE JUNIOR, J. F. **O Sentido dos Sentidos: a educagao do sensivel**. Curitiba: Edigoes Criar, 2001.

MERLEAU-PONTY, Maurice. **Phenomenology of Perception**. 2ª ed. Sao Paulo: Martins Fontes, 1999.

NUNES, Camila Xavier; REGO, Nelson. **The geographies of the body and sensible education in geography teaching.** In: Revista Brasileira de Educagao em Geografia, Rio de Janeiro, v. 1, n. 1, p. 86-107, jan./jun., 2011.

SANTIN, Silvino. **Physical education**: **a philosophical approach to corporeality**. Ijui: UNIJUI, 1987.

. **Physical education: Pedagogical themes**. Porto Alegre, EST/ESEF, 1992.

. **Physical Education: from the joy of playfulness to the oppression of performance. Porto Alegre:** Edigoes EST/ESEF - UFRGS, 1994.

SERRES, Michel. **Mestiga Philosophy**. Rio de Janeiro: Nova Fronteira, 1993.

## 2 PLAY AND CHILDREN'S PHYSICAL EDUCATION: A REPORT ON A PEDAGOGICAL EXPERIENCE AT UFRN'S NUCLEO DE EDUCAGAO DA INFANCIA (NEI).

Erika Janaina Santiago Moreira Freire
Master's student PPGEF-UFRN/NEI.erikafreire@outlook.com.br

Aguinaldo Cesar Surdi
Teacher from DEF/UFRN.aguinaldosurdi@yahoo.com.br

## INTRODUCTION

We can undoubtedly say that play is part of human nature, as well as the culture we live in and education. In this understanding, play is an essential element to be incorporated into educational practices at school. However, it can be seen that historically, in the theoretical-methodological proposals for teaching in traditional Physical Education, this thinking was not considered. However, with the revolution of the new teaching concepts of the renewal movement in the 1980s, the understanding of play began to be sown by the fields of knowledge of the body, culture and education, reaching a critical point of view with regard to the pedagogical proposal of schools.

Play in the educational process has motivated and continues to motivate a large group of scholars. Piaget (1994) emphasized the idea that children are explorers who use experience to build their knowledge. In this way, playful activities are fundamental, because they provide opportunities for pleasure, thus favoring interaction with the physical and social environment. Erickson (1950), in turn, comments that it is through play that the child conquers the environment. He invests in this process because it is filled with joy and provides pleasure. Froebel (2001) also attaches great importance to free activities, valuing the child's freedom of expression, which can happen through spontaneous play.

From this point of view, play in children's Physical Education has a formative intent, which is intertwined with the imaginative, expressive, sensitive and creative capacities of those involved. It presents itself as a possibility in the construction of knowledge, corresponding to an artistic process that allows children to experience their bodies in different dimensions of feeling, contributing to the construction of new knowledge and bodily actions. An education that affirms itself in experience, in feeling with others and in feeling. At this juncture, we contemplate aesthetic experiences that involve perceiving, knowing and understanding the world, allowing us to seek teaching that permeates the (re)meaning of self and other in an esthesiological form of human existence. Grouped into movements, play brings together expressiveness, language, imagination, experience, perception, manifestation, senses, meanings, creation, presence, the sensitive... These terms arise from the simple and at the same time complex PLAY! In the words of Capistrano (2005, p.108), through the language of play, children learn, re-signify the world, "[...] by gesturing, drawing, singing, telling stories, dancing, modeling, etc.

With the aim of reflecting on the practice of play and its importance at school, an experience report was drawn up on play in Early Childhood Physical Education classes at the Nucleo de Educagao da Infancia (NEI), Coldgio de Aplicacao (CAp) of the Universidade Federal do Rio Grande do Norte (UFRN), anchored in the research theme and the principles of art teaching adopted by the school, which is guided by Ana Mae Barbosa's Triangular Approach. In this way, we consider it pertinent to share some of the experiences that have taken place and which may subsidize other reports of experiences, as well as new research, which may enable new or different interpretations of the importance of thinking about play at school.

## PLAY AND SOME CONSIDERATIONS ABOUT ITS PRESENCE AND IMPLICATION AT SCHOOL

From the primitive era to contemporary times, play has been present in society, whether as a moment to explore the unknown, the imaginary, to exchange knowledge of oneself and others - in short, it is the incorporation of the symbolic act through experiences with the simple fact of existing in the world. Based on this, authors have dedicated themselves to studying the existence of play throughout history, and there is unanimity when it comes to stating that it has been part of human life since the beginning of its existence (VYGOTSKY, 1991; FRIEDMANN, 1996; BROUGERE, 1998; DOHME, 2002).

As Marin and Penon (2003/2004, p. 30) point out, "...play is the main activity of childhood. It responds to the need of boys and girls to look, touch, satisfy their curiosity, experiment, discover, express, communicate, dream... Play is a need, a primal and free impulse that drives us from an early age to discover, get to know, master and love the world and life." In this sense, it doesn't just manifest itself as random movements, play provides expression, communication, experimenting and interacting with their own body, with others and also with the various objects present in the world. In this line of thought, play at school will appear as an essential element in the educational formation of subjects.

According to Doherty, apud Surdi (2010), play allows babies and young children to learn about themselves and the world around them; they don't separate play from learning or any other moment. So play is their learning and vice versa. When children play, they imagine, and so they are able to overcome and transform reality. They are able to express themselves through a global perception of reality, which allows this perception to always be new, creative and full of learning, in which reality is constantly reinvented.

Play reveals the child's way of being. All the symbolism used by the child in the act of playing is global. Winnicott (1975, p.80) says that "it is in play, and only in play, that the individual, child or adult, can be creative and use his integral personality". Children are able to organize their world through the symbolic power of creation. Everything becomes possible in play. The sensitive dimensions become interconnected with everything that happens around them. Nothing is lost. Everything has meaning and significance. In play, the child's playful sensitivity allows them to fantasize about their creatures and their names and that, at any moment, everything can change and have another meaning. There is no such thing as being wrong. What exists are different possibilities for play, with which the child momentarily alters their world so that it has different meanings. In doing so, they intensify their imaginative and creative power in the face of their world, organizing it bodily in a calm and safe manner. Santin (1994, p.33) comments that the corporeality of playful activity is

> [...] like the sonority of a musical instrument. Sound is inseparable from the instrument itself, and sound cannot be separated from melody. The melodic body is formed by the voices of a choir or the sounds of an orchestra. Voices and sounds cannot be separated from people and musical instruments. Voices, sounds, people and musical instruments form a whole with the melody. Play forms a unique and indivisible bodily sensibility, and the melody of the corporeality of play is called joy.

It can be seen that, as a school practice, play has been far from legislated for a long time, nor does it appear explicitly in the 1988 Federal Constitution, a historical moment in which early childhood education was doubly protected as a subjective right of children (art. 208, IV) and as a right of urban and rural workers (art. 7, XXV). This situation is also reinforced in Law 9.394/96, which regulates early childhood education as the first stage of basic education. It is addressed more directly when the right to play is mentioned, in art. 29 of this Law, which states that "the integral development of children up to 5 (five) years of age is ensured, in its physical, psychological, intellectual and social aspects, complementing the action of the family and the community (Redaction given by Law No. 12.796, of 2013)" (Brasil, 2013). In light of these aspects, it can be seen that despite the absence in the laws mentioned of the right to play in Early Childhood Education, they were fundamental in that they legally ensured children's right to full development at this educational stage.

In the Statute of Children and Adolescents - ECA (Law No. 8.069/1990), the right to play is expressed in a more contemplative way. Article 16 of the ECA includes the right to freedom as the right to "play, practice sports and have fun" (Brasil, 1990). In 2009, the MEC reworked the document "Criteria for childcare that respects children's fundamental rights", originally published in 1995, which established the right to play as the first criterion for a childcare center that effectively respects children. In the same year, the National Curriculum Guidelines for Early Childhood Education (Resolution No. 5, of December 17, 2009 - Establishes the National Curriculum Guidelines for Early Childhood Education), which establishes that pedagogical proposals must guarantee, among other children's rights...the right to play.

Among other aspects measured, the child's right to movement and movement in internal and external spaces, both in the reference room and in the institution. It also adds that the institution should provide toys and equipment that are in keeping with the specific characteristics of local communities, suggesting that pedagogical practices should be based on interaction and play in order to integrate the various experiences of children at this stage of education.

In 2014, the National Education Plan (Law No. 13.005) does not explicitly refer to the right to play, but preserves the specificities of early childhood education in item 13 of the first goal, referencing other documents mentioned above. In view of these achievements in the law, it is necessary to point out that the terms about play in the law are not explicitly about the act of playing, as it is often portrayed as a toy or a game. A toy is an object constructed primarily by the adult, offered to the child; it can also be constructed by children in their relationship when they play. This leads us to think that play doesn't necessarily depend on the toy, nor does the toy necessarily trigger play. These two concepts guide the act of playing and converge with the same intention. In view of these ideas, I support Vygotsky's (2003) understanding of play: the child is able, through the objects used in play, to establish explanations that differentiate the perceptual and symbolic fields.

## THE EARLY CHILDHOOD EDUCATION CENTER - NEI

The Early Childhood Education Center was created as a Supplementary Unit by Resolution 55/1979 - COSUNI, of May 17, 1979. Originally named the Nucleo Educacional Infantil, its initial purpose was to act as a crèche for the female university community - employees, students and teachers of the UFRN, receiving children from the age of 3 months. This project, however, was made unfeasible by the high costs that the infrastructure of a crèche would entail, so the nucleus was defined as a pre-school and began operating on June 4, 1979, serving children in the age range of 1 year and 8 months to 2 years and 6 months to 5 years and 11 months old. In 2008, it was extended to the general community.

In 2002, it was regulated by Resolution No. 002, of January 15, 2002, of the Teaching, Research and Extension Council - CONSEPE. It currently operates as a School of Application, linked to the Federal University of Rio Grande do Norte (UFRN) and the Education Center (CE), and is dedicated to Early Childhood Education (nursery and pre-school) and Primary Education (literacy cycle). In 2013, by means of Resolution 13/2013, of October 18, 2013, this school community welcomed the children and staff of the Unidade Educacional Infantil-UEI/UFRN, thus expanding its services.

The Childhood Education Unit - NEI/CAp-UFRN is based on the assumption that the formation, learning and development of the child in the school and social context is linked to the political and pedagogical role assumed by the institution as mediator-dynamizer of the relationship between the child's experiences and knowledge and the knowledge accumulated socially by humanity; and the participation and support of the family in the political and pedagogical management of the school. In order to assume this role, it defines a set of theoretical principles on the basis of which curricular activities are structured.

In its more than 30 years of existence, it has expanded its teaching offer to basic education, with the implementation of Primary Education in 2010; it began its journey in Research, and in Extension, investing in teacher training actions (Refresher Courses, Specialization Courses and the organization of Seminars and Educational Meetings).

The aim of Early Childhood Education at NEI-CAp/UFRN is to contribute effectively to ensuring that children are cared for according to their specific needs (of color, gender, social class or special educational needs), in an environment of respect and cooperation, allowing them to broaden their knowledge of themselves and the world - learning about oral language, writing, mathematics, science, theater, cultural traditions, music, play, dance, cinema, values, plastic arts, etc. This space provides opportunities for interaction between children and their peers, between them and adults, allowing them to experience and build affective relationships and attitudes of cooperation, autonomy and responsibility.

## THE EXPERIENCE OF PLAY IN CHILDREN'S PHYSICAL EDUCATION CLASSES

In childhood, play is a natural and cultural manifestation of the human body. As Baitelo Junior (2001, p. 2) states

> The body blossoms in a thousand ways, unfolds in a thousand simultaneous languages, speaks a symphony of messages in every attitude. And it builds a history that is not just the history of the species - but encompasses it -, that is not just the history of its time - but encompasses it, - that is not just the history of its individual life journey - but also portrays it. A history that is not only the memory of a past, but also the mirror of a future, with its dreams, projects, utopias, plans, desires and aspirations.

In our immense desire to contribute to a more humane, emancipated and sensitive formation of children in Physical Education classes at the NEI, we sought to assume a pedagogical position to this end; since when we say that play leads us to seek to contribute to educational formation in the sensitive language of the world. It is through play that the body shows us its presence in the world, so that we can understand it and give it meaning. Our existence is realized in the body (MERLEAU-PONTY, 1999).

With this, we find that [...] teaching does not transfer knowledge, but creates the possibilities for its own production or construction" (FREIRE, 1996, p.47). Educating must be seen as a continuous process, in which the subjects involved are not mere spectators, but active subjects, who create and (re)create meanings and transform themselves and others in their experiences with the world.

With the intention of working towards a "subject body", i.e. proposing an artistic experience in which the children would have the opportunity not only to follow the axes of children's Physical Education, but also to recreate their repertoire of learned movements, we set ourselves the challenge of providing a link between theory and practice in the pedagogical actions of Physical Education classes.

In an attempt to broaden a view of the teaching of Early Childhood Physical Education, to promote new body possibilities during pedagogical practices, it proposes an approximation of play/education. From this perspective, the body and movement installation was one of the experiences lived by the children in class 2 during the period from September 13 to December 13, 2016; in other words - the 3rd school term - during the development of the "Babies" Research Theme.

The research theme is the methodology adopted by NEI/CAp- UFRN since the 1980s to articulate three basic dimensions of the educational experience: the culturally constituted knowledge in different fields that we want to make available, the children's experiences, i.e. the children's socio-cultural context or their immediate reality, and the aspects linked to learning and development. A research topic usually arises from the children's curiosity about a certain subject. This curiosity takes over their whole body and they demand space to express themselves, whether orally, in drawings or gestures. This is what happened with the topic in question: the teachers in class 2 observed the children's curiosity about the female human body, because there were some mothers in the class who were pregnant... expecting their second child. This sparked a global curiosity in the class and the children showed a collective interest in the baby. When asked what they would like to know about this topic, the children wanted to find out why and how babies appear, grow and move. From this comes the awakening of the body itself, as well as the bodies of others. Thus, the movement of the body became a greatness to be explored by the children in this research topic. There were several experiences to broaden the children's repertoire around the question "what makes a baby's body move?", including the construction of the "Body and movement" installation.

This experience was initially based on the principles of art teaching adopted by the NEI, which is guided by the Triangular Approach. This is a contemporary trend in art teaching systematized in Brazil by researcher Ana Mae Barbosa (BARBOSA, 2009). This approach proposes that individuals approach art by observing the actions of reading, contextualizing and making. These actions should not be seen separately, but as a spiral in constant interaction. Reading refers to the attribution of meanings to images, from art or everyday life, which occurs in the dialogue between the reader and the text to be read, through the aesthetic analysis of these productions. Contextualizing involves the aesthetic and experiential universe that surrounds the image, it involves seeing the culture that surrounds art, it involves the plurality of this culture that can be reconstructed in various ways, and not just through historical narrative. In making, the expressive dimension emerges in a creative process that is both personal and cultivated. It's personal because the child is faced with the challenge of giving form to their thoughts, feelings and desires, and cultivated because this process is always being enriched by cultural information (contextualization) and by reading images.

The Physical Education classes in nursery school, in class 2, are for children who are between 3 and 4 years old, and point to the importance of experiences that make it possible to experience play in its diversity of manifestations with the body in a spontaneous way. In this sense, the Physical Education classes were designed and planned through the construction of knowledge about the research topic. With this in mind, we began interactive and creative pedagogical actions between the children and the teacher. Thus, some of the aspects necessary for the formation of the students' sensibility, indicated by these proposals, such as composition, appreciation and artistic fruition, remain in dialog with fundamental elements for the artistic process, such as creation, imagination and sensitivity.

In the first Physical Education lesson, the initial conversation established an interaction with the content already begun with the teachers in class. When the conversation turned to the formative process of babies through *fertilization,* the initial proposal was to think about what it would be like to race to the woman's ovum, with the children being the sperm - we put a ribbon on the children's clothes simulating the tail of the sperm. After inserting the tape into the clothes, we delimited the space to the end of the court and when we touched the protective net, the children would have reached their goal. The next moment, we rethought the fact that the ovum is a smaller space than the court, so we delimited the space into an arc to carry out the activity, allowing them to pass through this new space bodily. The experience of this activity was designed in an organized and interactive way with each group - pre-established - in order to avoid the frustration of some by not carrying out the activity, as well as avoiding bodily encounters in this delimited space. Waiting at this stage is also not positive.

Photo: September 16, 2016.

Gradually, the new space and the children realize the interface between play and education, emerging into new bodily possibilities as they are involved in a collective experience that spreads pleasure and joy through the manifestation of the body. "The child has a different balance, and it is necessary to treat child consciousness as a positive phenomenon". (MERLEAU PONTY, 2006, p.65)

In the second meeting, the previous lesson was taken up again and this meeting of the sperm and the ovum, i.e. fertilization, was projected once more. After this meeting, we moved on to the process of *forming the fetus* in the mother's belly. We began by imagining the grouping of cells after fertilization, and asked the children to divide into groups in the space of an arch to create this fetus. Then we asked them to organize themselves so that each one could stay in this space, imagining how the fetus stays there. Then they were given other arches, allowing everyone to explore these movements. It is at this moment that play puts us into the world through understanding ourselves and existing through our bodies.

In the third meeting, the Physical Education class aimed to understand the *fetus and its growth in the mother's belly*. With the arches projected onto the floor, we asked the children to each express, through their bodies, their way of thinking about how the fetus is growing and developing in this space, i.e. in the mother's belly. In this way, they give themselves over to the sensible, enabling all bodily expression, feelings and manifestations, without, however, sticking to rigid patterns of movement. Merleau-Ponty (1999) also defends the idea that all scientific knowledge is based on sensitive knowledge, because our body and the world are linked as an indivisible substance. Play becomes something inherent to be explored in order to propose aesthetic and artistic situations which, by expanding the children's perceptions and observations as well as their repertoires of knowledge.

Following on from the lessons, we were able to *experience the children (babies) in their mother's belly feeding* through the umbilical cord, among other body movements that are made, such as: involuntary movements, waking up, sleeping, kicking, squirming, among others that the children themselves spoke about...

Photo: September 27, 2016

In the following meeting, we take up some of the movements that were experienced and make it possible for *this baby to be born*, leaving this space of sensations and comfort to live new experiences. It is at this moment that we awaken to expressiveness through a concept of rupture, of breaking away from the surrounding world - into the world that emerges through body experience.

Another important point was the presentation of the *different* births that take place when a baby is born. And at this moment, the children, in a unified and expressive way, began the process of (re)creation, meaning and senses of this moment passed by the baby.

Photo:October 04, 2016

Based on the assumptions and methodologies of these concepts, we tried to provide the children with different experiences. Through pedagogical processes, they were encouraged to discover and experiment with different ways of "moving" (KUNZ, 2001). This allowed the children to experience the symbolic world and broaden their perceptual experiences, always attributing meaning and significance to their creations, finding different forms of expression in the act of playing.

The Physical Education classes continued their research into the walking and running motor skills of these babies, based on the assumption that this is the time these children experience in the process of growing up. The experience of playing is characterized here as the experimentation of movements based on the movement intentions that were brought up as problem situations and that there was no pre-established movement model and the children, based on their own movement repertoire, were able to explore their bodies and through it construct and deconstruct their learning, re-elaborating, unfolding and transforming the movements into creations and new creations, as well as artistic appreciation.

## FINAL CONSIDERATIONS

Physical education classes in early childhood education provide children with the opportunity to return to their human essence, bring them closer to the natural environment in which they live, as well as presenting challenges and overcoming natural obstacles through movements that are adjusted by the environment and through their body culture.

In this sense, the approach to the theme of babies allows us, together with the children of the NEI/CAp nursery school, to experience and appreciate this bodily practice and understand the culture of movement, based on the conception of the body, nature and culture, which are intertwined with the knowledge of play, children's imagination, or better still, spontaneous knowledge related to the children's reality, with the aim of stimulating a critical reading of the body manifestations learned, and the possibilities of establishing connections with other cultures, bringing them closer to different realities, so that they can interact and exchange knowledge with the body.

Finally, it also allows us to intertwine play with education and provokes the awakening of being - while doing and living - through organic changes. In this sense, it is possible to see that school physical education in early childhood education leads us to a social and pedagogical practice that produces senses and meanings for children, so that they can interact with their bodies, their nature and their culture in a spiral of knowledge that is intrinsically rooted in the world.

## BIBLIOGRAPHICAL REFERENCES


BAITELLO Jr., N. **O corpo e suas linguagens** In: OPENING CONFERENCE OF THE FIRST INTERNATIONAL COLOQUIUM ON THE BODY/CONSCIOUSNESS. 1; 2001 Natal. Proceedings...Natal p. 1-8.

BARBOSA, Ana Mae Tavares Bastos. **The image in art teaching:** 1980s and new times. 7ª ed. rev. Sao Paulo: perspectiva, 2009.

BRAZIL / Ministry of Education and Culture. **Criteria for childcare that respects children's fundamental rights**. Brasilia: MEC, 1995

BRAZIL. Presidency of the Republic. 1988 Constitution. **Constitution of the Federative Republic of Brazil**: promulgated on October 5, 1988. Brasilia, DF.

BRASIL. **Lei de Diretrizes e Bases da Educação Nacional**. n° 9.394 de dezembro de 1996. Brasilia: Chamber of Deputies, 1996.

BRAZIL. **Statute of Children and Adolescents**. Federal Law No. 8069, of July 13, 1990. Rio de Janeiro: Official Press, 2002.

BRAZIL. Ministry of Education. National Education Council. **CEB Resolution no. 05**, Dec. 17, 2009. Diario Oficial Republica Federativa do Brasil, Brasilia, DF, Dec. 18, 2009.

BROUGERE, G. **Play and education.** Porto Alegre: Artes Medicas. 1998.

CAPISTRANO, N. J. Motricidade, cultura de movimento e o brincar. In: MELO, J. P. de; PONTES, G. M. D. de; CAPISTRANO, N. J. (Orgs). **Teaching Art and Physical Education in Childhood.** Natal: UFRN/Padeia/MEC, 2005b. p. 106-113.

DOHME, V. A. **Playful activities in education:** the yellow brick road of learning. Master's dissertation. Postgraduate course in Education, Art and Cultural History. Mackenzie Presbyterian University. Sao Paulo. 2002.

FREIRE, J.B. ***Educagao de Corpo Inteiro***. Sao Paulo: Scipione, 1996.

FRIEDMANN, A. **O direito de brincar: a brinquedoteca**. 4ª ed. Sao Paulo: Abrinq, 1996.

FROEBEL. Friedrich A. **The Education of Man**. Passo Fundo: UPF, 2001.

MARIN, I.; PENON, S. Which toy to choose? **Revista Patio Educagao Infantil**, ano I, n. 3, p. 29-31, dez. 2003/mar. 2004.

MERLEAU-PONTY, M. Fenomenologia da percepgao. 2nd ed. Sao Paulo: Martins Fontes, 1999.

. **Psychology and pedagogy of children**: Sorbonne courses (1949-1952). Trad. Ivone Benedetti. Sao Paulo: Martins Fontes, 2006.

KUNZ, Elenor. **Physical Education:** teaching & change. Ijui: Unijul, 2001.

PIAGET, Jean. **Six studies in psychology**. 20th ed. Rio de Janeiro: Forense Universitaria, 1994.

SANTIN, Silvino. **Physical Education: from the joy of playfulness to the oppression of performance. Porto Alegre:** Edigoes EST/ESEF - UFRGS, 1994.

SURDI, Aguinaldo Cesar. **Physical Education and Meaningful Human Movement:** a Phenomenological Possibility. Videira, SC: Exito, 2010.

WINNICOTT, Donald Woods. **Play and reality**. Rio de Janeiro: Imago, 1975.

VYGOTSKI, Lev Semenovich. The role of play in development. Sao Paulo: Martins Fontes. 2003.

Accessed on December 13, 2016:

http://www.planalto.gov.br/ccivil03/Ato2011-2014/2014/Lei/L13005.htm-

http://www.planalto.gov.br/ccivil 03/Ato2011-2014/2013/Lei/L12796.htm-

# 3 PHYSICAL EDUCATION IN EARLY CHILDHOOD EDUCATION: CAPOEIRA - AN INTERTWINING OF KNOWLEDGE

Ana Flavia Gomes da Cunha
Fellow of NEI/UFRN.anaflaviagomes03@hotmail.com

Debora Sarah Dantas da Silva
Teacher at NEI/UFRN.deboradd.sarah@gmail.com

Erika Janaina Santiago Moreira Freire Master's student PPGEF-UFRN/NEI.erikafreire@outlook.com.br

## INTRODUCTION

> The important thing about school is not only to study, not only to work, but also to create friendships, to create an atmosphere of camaraderie, to socialize, and to 'stick to it'! It's logical [...] In a school like this, it will be easy to study, work, grow, make friends, educate yourself and be happy.
>
> (Paulo Freire)

The aim of this article is to enable teachers to reflect on their practice, providing knowledge of the diversity and complexity of school practice, given that the school is a place with a context that is differentiated by a set of movements, but with a defined socio-historical function as a transmitter of knowledge developed by humanity, made up of subjects who construct their knowledge by interacting with each other. It is through these interactions between the subjects of the school space (child/children, child/adult), the objects of knowledge and the mediation of language, that new learning is appropriated.

The corporal manifestation of capoeira was one of the experiences enjoyed by the children in class 4 in the first quarter of 2016 during the development of the Research Theme "Bale and Capoeira". In this context, the Physical Education classes with the specialist teacher had 4 (four) meetings in Early Childhood Education, which is taught by a single teacher (pedagogues).

From the perspective of our work, as mediating teachers, we recognize that the criangas have knowledge that goes beyond the school walls. The children brought with them knowledge about capoeira, and it was up to us, the teachers, to take it into account, organize it and expand it. From this understanding, we proposed teaching and learning activities about capoeira in which they were challenged in their possibilities, to advance and organize what they already knew, in situations that allowed them to interact with organized scientific knowledge about this dance.

As mediators of the study, we considered the knowledge built up by the children in their social relationships with their families, their friends and the world they belong to, and we encouraged the children to express their knowledge about A CAPOEIRA. We believe that by verbalizing, the children expose their own unique way of thinking (BRASIL, 1998). Based on the children's initial ideas and their interest in the respective study, we came up with some objectives in order to provide the children with capoeira experiences from a physical education perspective. In this sense, the children's learning took place in a contextualized way, in significant teaching-learning situations, as described below.

## CAPOEIRA AND PHYSICAL EDUCATION - CIRCULATING KNOWLEDGE IN EARLY CHILDHOOD EDUCATION

Physical Education is the school subject that prioritizes knowledge of the possibilities of using the body in the research topic "Capoeira" - specific content of the curricular component - is a bodily practice, which enables a circulating form of knowledge. Its bodily manifestation through movements and gestures presents sensations and experiences that allow children to develop a bodily organization that goes beyond the biological, in other words, an understanding that encompasses the cultural and historical at the same time. In this sense, we understand Physical Education as a social and pedagogical practice whose conception of teaching and learning is the Movement Culture approach.

This term has been used by Kunz since 1991 in Physical Education as an organizing criterion for school knowledge. The author seeks to overcome the reductionist view of Physical Education by re-dimensioning the concept of culture, and also aims to relate its meanings and intentionality to human movement. Supported by Dietrich, the author states that "Movement culture initially means a global conceptualization of cultural objectives, in which human movement becomes the element of symbolic intermediation and of meanings traditionally produced and maintained in certain communities or societies". (KUNZ, 2001, p.38)

The Physical Education classes in Early Childhood Education at NEI/CAp are a social and pedagogical practice that seeks the corporeality considered appropriate for children, structuring times and spaces for the body and mind, from an ontological perspective of being. Strictly speaking, it is the search for a sense of the totality of man in the modern contemporary world as a result of the culture present in the world of our existence.

Based on this understanding, the encounters with Physical Education provided the singularity of a historical-cultural and social being in capoeira through the transmission of knowledge that reveals knowledge that can understand the body in relation to its nature and culture, and the intertwining between them, which appears "one" in the sensible and intelligible knowledge of school Physical Education.

Given the above, we will take a look at the practice experienced in capoeira class 4 at NEI/CAp. We will report on the first meeting in order to sequence the appropriation of the process of interactions and relationships that were built, through which the children shared knowledge. In order to get the children to participate in the activities proposed by the teachers, as well as to make them experience the movements of the body in the body practice, the meeting with the class had as its central axis the initiation of the teaching - learning process through the teacher's previous survey with the children about the capoeira body practice: how it is defined and its relationship with history, clothing, instruments, the place - how it is done and some movements. To help us understand what capoeira is and how it is defined in different concepts. Adorno (1987) describes that:

> "Capoeira consists of a dance in which the use of risky movements - given the circumstance of camouflaging possible contention - involves the participants and infects those watching. The dual nature of fighting disguised as play gives shape to a game of movements combining objectivity and precision in attack with fast, original defenses, in which the body is used to the limit of the resources of muscular elasticity and flexibility, thus composing a beautiful human plasticity in stripped-down, natural gestures, in a strange dance of danger." (p.4)

With this in mind, capoeira is a cultural manifestation that brings together knowledge that was initially built up as a struggle of resistance, which throughout history has presented facets that go beyond dances, games, sports, gymnastics, fights that are sometimes part of it and sometimes separate.

By appropriating the children's previous knowledge in terms of historical aspects, as well as the cultural aspects already explained and worked on by the teachers in the classroom, the introduction of bodily movements was taken into account when carrying out practical activities. In this process of interaction and relationships, children are human beings in formation who are capable of constructing and (re)constructing senses and meanings associated with the imagination and play, so that this space encourages them to develop their way of acting and thinking about the world to which they belong. With this in mind, we began to carry out physical activities on the school playground. At first, we suggested the activity "tica - cocorinha", which aimed to make the movements playful, as well as seeking to associate capoeira body movements and step names with the proposed activity. In this game, the child chosen to be the tica would tap another child, and when he was tapped, he had to duck (cocorinha) and could only be saved when the other child passed his leg over him (half moon from the front).

In the second moment, the proposed activity would involve the basic capoeira movement (ginga), through which the capoeiristas would perform the other steps. We started the activity with a triangular display of bamboles on the floor, where the children performed the forward and backward movements inserted into this space. After creating the movement, we added the sound of improvised and verbal musicality - the musical expression emitted when capoeira is performed by the instruments used by the capoeiristas. Then it was suggested that the criangas in pairs do the ginga movement facing each other, and then the body movement of the front half was included alongside the ginga.

To finish off, the students had a big roda - a characteristic capoeira space, or rather, a place where collective construction takes place, providing social relations and assigning each member a role - and presented themselves in the middle of the roda, showing a movement they had learned in class as a manifestation of the body that had been incorporated into the experience. In the final roda, the students showed the names of the movements they had assimilated from capoeira, as well as their understanding of the body and its cultural manifestation, which comes from the behavior of defense and attack in an expressive language of gestures.

This report shows us in a significant way that capoeira in Early Childhood Physical Education develops circulating knowledge as a web of knowledge that allows us to interpret and recreate the concepts that are part of the understanding of bodily practices to the point of expressing through the body and in language the existence of what has been apprehended in an intrinsic relationship of sense and meanings that are circular with the world through the other, with their body, with their history and with their culture, manifesting a continuity of permanent construction.

## THE BODY IN MOVEMENT: BUILDING KNOWLEDGE ABOUT CAPOEIRA

The body plays a fundamental role in the process of acquiring knowledge, because it is through the body that children establish their relationship with the world. Children discover the possibilities of their own bodies, experiencing them as action and language (BRASIL, 1998).

We arranged for the Physical Education teacher to intervene with the children once a week. She watched videos about capoeira movements and played games, such as tica-cocorinha, a statue, and a "moving" story about Little Red Riding Hood using capoeira movements. Sewing the knowledge together, we read informative texts about capoeira to the children. In this sense, the children carried out activities related to their knowledge of the body in their experiences of capoeira movements.

As a continuation of the study of capoeira, we invited Josue - a contramestre[1]to talk to the children about the dance, contributing to the work that was already being done with the class and broadening their knowledge. Josue first showed the capoeira instruments, such as the pandeiro, berimbau and caxixi, as well as introducing us to some of the dance's moves and its

1 Boatswain means The one next to the master or his substitute; Below the master or the boss. Sourcehttp://venenodanoite.blogspot.com.br/2013/03/o-que-e-um-contramestre.html

origins. He then showed the criangas the capoeira moves.

At that moment we made some great discoveries! We learned that capoeira came from Angola, that its movements originated from the movements of animals and that to dance capoeira you have to have a pandeiro, caxixi and berimbau.

As a strategy to systematize our studies, we encouraged the group to build sculptures out of newspaper, representing capoeira moves. The children then made paper dolls, chose a capoeira movement and represented it in the sculptures.

Considering the importance of working with body movement, we proposed an activity for the children in which, as they listened to the music, they danced capoeira, performing the movements they had learned, freely. Bregolin and Bellini say:

> Dance in the context of Early Childhood Education doesn't have to be restricted to one format and can be experienced by all ages. These classes allow students to get to know their bodies and their own selves, as well as being able to interact with the environment and their classmates, along with the music, rhythms and melodies.

With this in mind, our studies on Capoeira were carried out in a joyful, pleasurable and fun way, with lots of games and body movements, rich moments which contributed significantly to the children's teaching and learning process, as well as broadening their knowledge.

So, to finish our study of Capoeira, the children created a choreography that culminated in the "Class 4's dangas bale and capoeira show", which was entitled by the children themselves. These were moments of construction and reconstruction in which they experimented with different movement possibilities.

## FINAL CONSIDERATIONS

The school, as a privileged place for the production and learning of culture, can experiment and create new ways of accessing and living with knowledge in the most different and diverse areas of knowledge. The need for transformation in the way of knowing, learning and doing requires changes both in the environment, in the spaces for learning and reflection, and in the need for new attitudes, collective spirit, artistic and pedagogical creativity.

We saw progress in this construction process with the inclusion of the Physical Education specialist in Early Childhood Education, when at the end of the study on capoeira, we noticed the children's satisfaction when they were delighted, saying that they already knew a lot about this dance: the emergence of capoeira, capoeira steps, as well as the demystification of the stereotype that only boys can do capoeira, but that everyone can do capoeira.

In this sense, we see a great deal of enthusiasm as a result of the lessons learned, and challenges are faced with joy and pleasure, "which gives us the certainty that the search for knowledge is not, for children, preparation for anything, but life here and now." Freire (1983, p. 50). It's about involving children in order to present body experiences for learning that has meaning and significance for the expansion of knowledge as subjects of the culture of movement at NEI/CAp - UFRN.

## BIBLIOGRAPHICAL REFERENCES

ADORNO, Camile. **THE ART OF CAPOEIRA**. Goiania: Kelps, 1997.

BRAZIL. Ministry of Education and Culture. Secretariat for Primary Education. **National Curriculum for Early Childhood Education.** Brasilia, 1998. Vol. 1, 2 and 3.

BREGOLIN , Bruna. BELLINI, Magda A. B. C. *Danga in Early Childhood Education: parents', teachers' and coordinators' perceptions of dance in this context.* University of Caxias do Sul - DO CORPO: Ciencias e Artes - v. 5 - n. 1 - 2015 Available at **http://www.ucs.br/etc/revistas/index.php/docorpo/article/viewFile/4003/2292**

FREIRE, Madalena. **A paixao de conhecer o mundo: relato de uma professora**. Rio de Janeiro: Paz e Terra, 1983.

KUNZ, E. *Educagao Fisica:* ensino & mudangas. Ijul: Unijul, 1991.

KUNZ, Elenor. **Physical Education: teaching and change**. 2 ed. Ijul: Unijul, 2001a.

Capoeira moves.www.youtube.com

# 4 LE PARKOUR AND PHYSICAL EDUCATION: A CORPORAL PRACTICE OF MOVEMENT CULTURE FOR CHILDREN

Erika Janaina Santiago Moreira Freire
Master's student PPGEF-UFRN, prof[a] NEI - NATAL.erikafreire@outlook.com.br

Aguinaldo Cesar Surdi
Professor at DEF/UFRN. aguinaldosurdi@yahoo.com.br

## INTRODUCTION

The book fair held at our school in 2016 was one of the activities of the extension project: *Reading, Literature and Childhood Education: do ensino a formacao de mediadores de leitura, an* extension action linked to the Education Center, the Childhood Education Nucleus (NEI), the College of Application (CAp) of the Federal University of Rio Grande do Norte (UFRN) and the Media Studies and Research Group, Leitura e Infancias (Reading and Childhood), which aims to promote initial and ongoing training sessions involving literary reading apprentices, NEI teachers, undergraduate students from Library Science, Literature and Pedagogy courses and the school community.

In this project, the book fair is conceived as a cultural event, involving the NEI/CAp team, children from nursery and elementary school and booksellers, with the focus on encouraging reading through the exchange and purchase of literary works, thus becoming a space for promoting reading, a way of broadening their literary repertoire without spending money. In addition, the book fair program offered participants workshops in music, theater and physical activities.

The music and movement workshops had their approaches built simultaneously with the aim of (co)relating them in a way that unified the children's knowledge on the proposed theme. In this context, the music workshop worked with the Pop musical style - a theme addressed by the elementary school research.

During this workshop, the children were able to watch video clips of nationally and internationally renowned pop singers. During this activity, they were shown the video clip of pop singer Madonna, who, in addition to presenting her music, showed images and body movements of Parkour/Free - Running performed by Sebastien Foucan, one of the practitioners and promoters of this body practice.

From this context, the movement workshop anchored in this theme - adventure body practices, especially Le Parkour, in Physical Education - was involved in order to present body experiences for meaningful learning and for broadening the movement culture of the children of NEI/CAp - UFRN.

## HISTORY OF PARKOUR - A BODY PRACTICE OF ADVENTURE

The 20th century town of Lisses, 27 kilometers away from the French capital, was the ideal setting for the emergence of one of the body practices that has revolutionized the city of Paris in recent years. When

> [...] a group of children, including David Belle and Sebastien Foucan, face a lack of leisure facilities outside school. Many of them come into contact with "traditional" sports in the school environment, such as Olympic gymnastics and martial arts, but outside of school they find a hostile environment for leisure activities. This group of young people then began to explore the playful potential of Lisses' urban facilities, jumping over railings, benches and monuments (MARQUES, 2010, p. 5).

The well-known City of Light and Love was being presented with a difference compared to other cities in the world. Along with its walls, railings, stairs and cars, they were accompanied by

[...] the role of the young body in the urban tangle. *Bodies designed* to move quickly and, a priori, ignoring urban obstacles. However, it wasn't just about youthful displays of courage, strength or even recklessness in relation to life. Those youthful bodies that were gaining notoriety mainly via the *internet* were themselves the result of a previous *agency*, a mixture of sporting, artistic and educational disciplines (idem, 4).

As a result, there was a widening of the body in relation to new possibilities of movement, since the existing methods did not take into account the desire for discoveries. In this context, Georges Hebdrt , [2]was a pioneer in the search for an understanding of the body - through the creation of the Natural Method after observing the Indians in nature in their daily activities and what they did with it to survive. Based on this perception, he established a series of ten exercises that were divided into groups:

[...] 1 - walking; 2 - running; 3- jumping; 4 - quadrupedal; 5 - climbing; 6 - balancing; 7 - lunges; 8 - transports; 9 - defense; 10 - swimming. For him, these 10 types of exercise, or "natural acts", can be used in their simple form, that is, added to activities linked to practical life and entertainment (HEBERT, 1941, p. 10 *apud* SOARES, 2003, p. 27).

The Natural Method then inspired Raymond Belle, a fighter in the French fire department, to create the *Parkours de Combattant*, used to rescue his comrades who were in danger on missions. He became a teacher of this method within the fire department, teaching it to others.

The benefits of fast, efficient and controlled movements were not fame, elegance or a "spiritual ascent", they were the difference between life and death. Such a tool was used to reach each other, to rescue, to escape when the need arose and to survive (STRAMANDINOLI; REMONTE; MARCHETTI, 2012, p 19).

In this context, Raymond appropriated Georges' motto: *'F.lre fort, pour etre utile[3]" and*

2 French physical education teacher who created the Natural Method.
3 From the French meaning "Be strong to be useful".

his son, David Belle, later continued his father's idea - who became the creator of Parkour.

Through his knowledge of some of *Combattant's* military *Parkours* methodologies, David brought these movements into the urban environment, making the street a place to imitate this bodily expression, but with a touch of imagination and creativity.

In this context, Yamakasi[4] was born, the name given to the first Parkour group. This body practice was disseminated around the world after several viewings on the internet, as well as the release of the film B13[5] - 13th District, whose main character was David Belle - the creator of Parkour. Sebastien Foucan, a former member of the Yamakasi group, realized that there were other possibilities of movement to be created, and obstacles to be explored in different ways, without worrying about the time used during the course. Making the most of the space available.

In this way, the Parkour *Free Running* style was also created. This new form of body movement devised by Foucan is perceived by many as a form of exhibitionism, which is unnecessary, since after it was created, *Free Running* opened the door to competitions between *Parkour* practitioners, something that didn't exist until then, and which is banned by a large number of those who want to maintain the roots of[6] , claiming that with competition, the spirit of altruism among practitioners is lost, since the only competition that exists is that of the individual against himself.

*Parkour* therefore has two ways of being experienced: in its initial form, with the philosophy of "Be strong to be useful", and in the philosophy of *Free Running,* in which practitioners can

4 It means: "Strong body, strong mind".

5 Paris, 2010. Faced with the inevitable rise in crime in some suburbs, the government authorizes the construction of an isolation wall around neighbourhoods classified as high risk. The worst of these is the 13th district, which is controlled by a crime boss, Taha (Dominique Dorol). An upstanding young punk, Lei'to (David Belle), is determined to put an end to his power. When Taha retaliates by kidnapping Leito's sister, Lola (Dany Verissimo), his brother tries to rescue her, but is betrayed by the head of the 13th district police station, who fears Taha's power. Leito ends up being arrested and Lola is held prisoner by Taha, who has put a collar on her as if she were a dog. After 6 months, a missile is stolen and agent Damien (Cyril Raffaelli) is given the almost impossible task of disarming it, as it is in district B13 and in Taha's possession. Damien has less than 24 hours to do this, because according to his boss, the missile will explode at the end of that time, killing millions of people. So Damien poses as a prisoner being transferred with Leito and they both "escape", but not all the truth is revealed. Available at: http://www.adorocinema.com/filmes/filme- 54107/.

6 Available at:
http://www.abpk.org.br/tag/competicao/,e also at:
http://www.abpk.org.br/tag/competicao/.

perform acrobatics while overcoming movements.

## LE PARKOUR AND MOVEMENT CULTURE: A CONCEPTION OF BODY, CULTURE AND NATURE

In contemporary times, the search for leisure and pleasure in bodily practices related to adventure activities has become a striking and evident feature in recent years. The inclusion of these activities in Physical Education is intrinsically related to rural and urban spaces, and they explore everything around them, as well as along the way in different ways, awakening the body, culture and nature to a diversity of movements that exorbitate the perception of the being and its interaction with the world.

Parkour has stood out as an urban adventure body practice that has a structuring relationship between the body and the city, and is part of the modern world. It is also evident in the movement of the body and nature, and its interaction with the environment in which it lives, which it passes through or passes over, exploring different environments that make it see risks as something to be faced in "... as natural a way as possible, using the obstacle as if it were part of your body[6] [7] ". For the ABPK - Associação Brasileira de Parkour (2016) it consists of:

> "Running, hanging, jumping, hanging, crawling... Parkour is an activity that develops these skills and gives the practitioner back the ability to move freely in their environment."

In the school environment in Physical Education classes, Parkour provides a manifestation of the body, culture and nature, which brings us back to Kunz's (1991) approach to movement culture, which has been propagated in this curricular component as an organizing criterion for school knowledge. Elenor Kunz's proposal seeks to overcome a reductionist view of the merely physical concept of human movement and considers that this is (co-)related to

7 Definition published on the ABPK (Brazilian Parkour Association) website Available at: www.abpk.org.br accessed on June 29, 2016.

movement through its cultural meanings and intentionality.

Mendes & Nobrega (2009, p.2) point out that Kunz problematizes the mechanistic conception of body and movement, in which the body is separate from the world, and seeks foundations in the phenomenological conception of body and movement, i.e. that the human being is inseparable from the world in which he lives.

The term "culture of movement" helps us to understand bodily acts as biopsychosociological phenomena, in other words, that amplify the meanings and senses of man as a whole and in his interaction with the world. This relationship leads us to understand the deep connection between the body and the world through the aspects that can signify different ways of being, be it our actions, feelings or senses.

Based on this understanding, we see Parkour as an expression of movement culture. In this context, we present in this practice the existence of the body and its bodily possibilities, which are diluted and (re)constructed in order to bring about change in the gaze of the beholder and the practitioner, in other words, both who perceive it as a means to be awakened and led to new forms of bodily knowledge. Thus, in every gesture, in every movement, Parkour stands out for being a practice that contemplates breaking away from the regimented, disciplined, conditioned and molded body in a perspective that brings us closer to our natural existence in the lived world.

This interpretation allows us to understand the body in Parkour through movements that express our being, our way of living, feeling and producing meanings in the body technique produced. It is in this understanding of the body and its relationship with the world that Capistrano (2010) points out that "Through the body, we make ourselves present in the world, we appropriate culture and produce it, we humanize ourselves. The body is constructed and deconstructed" (p.67).

The restructuring of these movements in Parkour brings us a new body awareness in re-education and in the way we perceive them in the conception of human nature. In order to understand nature and its relationship with the human being, Maurice Mearleau-Ponty (2000) makes the following statement: "Nature is an enigmatic object, an object that is not entirely an object; it is not entirely in front of us. It is our ground, not what is in front of us, but what sustains us" (p. 4).

In Parkour, nature is guided by the appropriation of the human body, a dynamic relationship of movements that goes through choreographic rehearsals in the quest to overcome and conquer obstacles through creation and (re)creation by moving, inverting and unbalancing bodies in unexplorable spaces through cultural manifestations - seeking to reconnect with the natural environment.

In this context, interaction with the body and nature also brings us back to an understanding of culture, which manifests itself through the primordial and historical memory of human beings and their communication with their surroundings. In this way, culture in Parkour establishes in the individuals of the human species a constant dialogue between nature and the body with its environment, and vice versa through their bodily manifestations of moments lived and forgotten with the purpose of rescuing and eternalizing beliefs and values for other generations of what the human being is capable of accomplishing.

This understanding makes us realize that this insertion of this practice does not only advocate the culture of the past, but is marked by the metamorphosis of different cultures and essentially the current one; and this does not prevent them from communicating. In the view of Baitello Junior (1999, p.18) it should be considered that: "Culture is the communicative macrosystem that permeates all manifestations and must be understood as such in order to understand individualized cultural manifestations."

Much more than it seems, the triad of body, nature and culture in Parkour has its legitimate meaning in its use and in the dynamics between them, which improve the body techniques that are inherent to the human being, which are lost in the course of our human trajectory, due to adaptations that arise in the course of the life cycle that is given to us by the world. It is a bodily practice of adventure which, through the culture of movement, allows us to recognize the singularities that exist in the human being, starting from the biological and its ramification with culture in the world. Assigning senses and meanings through body movements that seem very simple: walking, running, jumping, langar, climbing... and others; however, that make it possible to (re)discover a new perception of being and having a new body, in nature and in the culture of the world.

## DEVELOPMENT OF THE MOVEMENT WORKSHOP

Parkour plays an important role in Physical Education classes, based on the concept of movement culture - it points out new bodily possibilities for its practitioners to develop their bodies, their culture and nature, in other words, it helps to develop their personalities. Beanchi (2008) apud Stramandinali; Remonte; Marchetti (2012), says that:

> [...] the only 'competition' that fits within the Parkour philosophy is that of the practitioner against himself, overcoming physical obstacles (walls, railings), psychological obstacles (fear, insecurities) and social obstacles (acceptance by family, society), in addition to altruism (p. 16).

We did the Parkur experience over two days, in the movement workshop - covering Early Childhood Education and Elementary Education on the other day at NEI/Cap UFRN. In Early Childhood Education, we carried out this body practice through children's imagination, asking the children to imitate some animals with a variation of the tica[8]one of them would be chosen to be the chaser, who, imitating the lion, would chase the others, and when he touched another child, he would also become a lion and would help him, so that everyone would become a lion, valuing the expression of each person in the essence of their body, their culture and their nature in their movements.

> Students use language, at first, as an exercise in discovering the possibilities of the body to imitate or imprint and then discovering that those gestures and imprints can represent their perceptions, desires and feelings (MELO; CAPISTRANO, 2005, p. 15).

Next, we went back to the children's imagination and placed a rope on the ground so that the children could balance on it, doing their best not to step off the rope, as we were simulating a very high wall, which is what Parkour practitioners do, because it's a very high wall.

> [...] each culture has its own way of preserving these expressive resources of movement, with variations in the importance given to facial

8 An activity that can be called catching.

expressions, gestures and body postures, as well as the meanings attributed to them (BRASIL, 1998, p. 19).

We continued the workshop by jumping. First, we laid out a course with bamboo sticks, which the children jumped into. Then, at the end of the course, we set up a standing bamboo pole so that the children could jump through it. Then we placed benches where the children would jump and land on the nearby mat, but when they landed, they would put their hands on the floor. We pointed out that this would help to cushion the fall, and we used the movement of a cat or a frog as an example at the time of the demonstration.

Photo: Students performing a precision jump.

This was the most fun activity, as the children wanted to keep jumping off the bench with each new attempt. "Curiosity stimulates children to want to do. The process of learning through curiosity allows knowledge to be incorporated. The body can generate experimentation that will empower the individual in the face of the task". (PEREIRA; ARMBRUST, 2010, p. 24).

In elementary school, we introduced the children to the history of Parkour, the types of clothing and the places where they can practice it, and the places where traucers [9]usually train in the city of Natal.

9 Name given to boys who practice Parkour. In the case of moças, it's called traucese.

[10]In the movement workshop, we used movements common to the children, "[...] the body is the body lived by the subject" (ORLANDI, 2014, p. 78), in other words, with the activity of chasing along the line, where the children could only move along the lines of the court. When they got tired, we limited the area so that more children could be chased.

Next, we place some obstacles forming a square in the center of the court, then we carry out another variation of the chase, the prisoner chase, in which the activity will be similar, but all the others who are caught will be taken into the square, however, they must jump over the obstacles together. And to free the "prisoners", those who are "free" would jump in, taking them by the hand and both jumping to the outside of the square. Parkour "develops a wide range of motor skills, as well as good motor, physical and psychological skills, and social responsibility towards others" (GAMA, 2008a apud STRAMANDINALI; REMONTE; MARCHETTI, 2012, p. 16).

The next activity was the precision jump[11] , jumping off the bench and landing on a mat on the ground. All the children were able to perform the movement several times, while we increased the distance to be reached. Many felt brave, while others were afraid they wouldn't make it, as their classmates were getting further with each attempt.

But "[...] fear, self-confidence, self-esteem, courage, insecurity, among others, are part of a *tracer's* daily life" (BEANCHI, 2008 apud STRAMANDINALI; REMONTE; MARCHETTI, 2012, p. 22). With this, we can see that:

> [...] in addition to practicing skills in real situations, it can simulate dangerous situations, developing skills in both the motor and cognitive spheres, because in this way, by taking risks, even if in a controlled way, the student will have to solve problems that, among other things, will exercise their reaction time, initiative and speed of adaptation, characteristics that stimulate a critical attitude and decision making (ALVES; CORSINO, 2013, p.254).

Moving on to the next "challenge", we learned how to climb the wall. We went to a space next to the court, where there is a structure about 90 cm high. Before we started, we checked that the area was suitable for use, that there were no thorns, sharp objects, etc.

10 Activity that consists of moving only on the lines.
11 Jumping from one point to another.

> [...] when a *tracer* encounters a physical obstacle, before executing any movements, they evaluate three types of restrictions: the individual (ability to perform the movement); the task (level of complexity); and the environment (new environment or one they are already used to). All these items are assessed to ensure safety and the best execution of the movement (BEANCHI, 2008 apud STRAMANDINALI; REMONTE; MARCHETTI, 2012, p. 22).

In the same way, "Parkour practitioners see opportunities that involve jumps, different, original movements" (CARVALHO, 2008 apud STRAMANDINALI; REMONTE; MARCHETTI, 2012, p. 16), and the children were able to experience this. Next, we returned to the court and placed various obstacles around the court, where the students initially saw the teacher demonstrate one of the possibilities for overcoming the obstacles.

Afterwards, they went through the route, performing the movements in the way they could and also using their creativity, which arises from a curiosity that we may have: "will this movement work?", because:

> As a teacher, I have to know that without the curiosity that moves me, that makes me restless, that inserts me into the search, I can neither learn nor teach. Exercising my curiosity correctly is a right that I have as a person and that corresponds to the duty to fight for it, the right to curiosity (ASSMANN 2004, p. 192 apud FREIRE 1996, p. 85).

It can thus be a stimulant and generator of creativity, providing new visions of the space in front of them, generating other possibilities. In this way, the children were building a swallow by interpreting the obstacles they encountered, because according to Orlandi (2014):

> Parkour is this mixture in which we distinguish between what is an object and what is a gesture of interpretation of the object, which transforms it as a constitutive part of the movement narrated by the body that gives it, and makes sense of it. The body-narrative brings its meaning to the Parkour swallow. The body and its swallowing (p. 81).

Therefore, the body is a guiding principle of body practice and this, within the school, leads both to the human condition of living, as well as collaborating with the construction of a school that stands out for its commitment to teaching for life - contaminating with the formative and provocative actions of culminating and pleasurable experiences with corporeality.

## FINAL CONSIDERATIONS

The body practice related to the adventure activity in focus - Le Parkour - as a content of School Physical Education that is emerging today that can provide children with the search for a return to the human essence, bring them closer to the natural environment in the world in which they live, as well as present challenges and overcome natural obstacles through movements that are being adjusted by the environment and through their body culture.

In this sense, Parkour has enabled the children of NEI/CAp in nursery school and elementary school to experience and appreciate this bodily practice and understand the culture of movement, based on the concept of the body, nature and culture, which are intertwined with the knowledge of play, children's imagination, or better still, spontaneous knowledge related to the children's reality, with the aim of stimulating a critical reading of the body manifestations learned, and the possibilities of establishing connections with other cultures, bringing them closer to different realities, so that they can interact and exchange knowledge with the body, its nature and its culture.

The educational practice of Parkour allows an understanding of the culture of movement, and causes the awakening of the being - while doing and living - in addition to organic changes. In this sense, it is possible to see that School Physical Education is a social and pedagogical practice that produces senses and meanings for children, so that they can interact with their bodies, their nature and their culture in an interweaving of entirely new knowledge that is established with the lived world.

# BIBLIOGRAPHICAL REFERENCES


ALVES, Carla da Silva Reis; CORSINO, Luciano Nascimento. Parkour as a possibility for School Physical Education. **Motrivivencia Magazine - Year XXV, N° 41, P. 247 - 257 Dec./2013.**

ASSMANN, Hugo. **Curiosity and the pleasure of learning.** - Petropolis, RJ: Vozes, 2004 (Chapters 6 and 7).

BAITELLO JUNIOR, N. Machine syndrome. In: Castro, G.de. et all. (eds). **Essays on complexity**. Porto Alegre: Sulina, 1997.p.115-121.

BRAZIL, Ministry of Education and Sports. Department of Basic Education. **Referencial curricular nacional para a educagao infantil** / Ministdrio da Educagao e do Desporto, Secretaria de Educagao Fundamental. - Brasilia: MEC/SEF, 1998. 3v.: ill.

CAPISTRANO, Naire Jane. Physical education and early childhood education: In .
The Pedagogical Place
da Educagao na Educagao Infantil: Saberes (re) construuldos na formacao continuada do Paiddia/UFRN. 2010.p 51-81.

MARQUES, Rafael Adriano. **Ludic City:** an anthropological study of Parkour practices in Sao Paulo. 2010. 87 f. Dissertation (Master's Degree) - Faculty of Philosophy, Letters and Human Sciences, Department of Anthropology, University of Sao Paulo, Sao Paulo, 2011. (Chap. 1). Available at: <http://www.teses.usp.br/teses/disponiveis/8/8134/tde-05072011-142133/pt-br.php>.

KUNZ, E. **Physical Education:** teaching & changes. Ijui: Unijul, 1991.

MENDES, Maria Isabel Brandao de Souza; NOBREGA, Terezinha Petrucia. **Body and culture of movement:** reflections on the relationship between body, nature and culture. Rev. Pensar a pratica, vol. 12, n° 2, p. 1-10, May/Aug. 2009.

MERLEAU- PONTY, M. **Nature:** notes: courses at the Colldge de France. Translated by Alvaro Ribeiro de Moura. Sao Paulo: Martins Fontes, 1999.

ORLANDI, Eni Puccinelli. Parkour: body and space rewrite the subject. **Linguas e Instrumentos Linguisticos Magazine - N° 34 - jul - dec 2014.**

STRAMANDINOLI, A. L. M.; REMONTE, J. G. MARCHETTI, P. H. Parkour: history and concepts of the sport. **Mackenzie Journal of Physical Education and Sport - v. 11, n. 2, 2012.**

PEREIRA, Dimitri Wuo; ARMBRUST, Igor. **Pedagogy of Adventure:** Extreme, adventure and action sports at school. Jundiai/SP: Ed. Fontoura, 2010.

SOARES, Carmen Lucia. **Georges Hebert and the Natural Method:** new sensibility, new education of the body. Revista Brasileira de Ciencias e Esportes. Campinas, v. 25, n. I, p. 21-39, sep, 2003.

# I want morebooks!

Buy your books fast and straightforward online - at one of world's fastest growing online book stores! Environmentally sound due to Print-on-Demand technologies.

Buy your books online at
**www.morebooks.shop**

Kaufen Sie Ihre Bücher schnell und unkompliziert online – auf einer der am schnellsten wachsenden Buchhandelsplattformen weltweit! Dank Print-On-Demand umwelt- und ressourcenschonend produzi ert.

Bücher schneller online kaufen
**www.morebooks.shop**

info@omniscriptum.com
www.omniscriptum.com

Printed by Books on Demand GmbH, Norderstedt / Germany